Safety Tips

Being safe when you travel is important. Remember to:

-Make sure you can see the adult you're with

-Set a meeting place in case you cannot find your adult

-Know your adult's phone number - write it here:

-If you feel lost, ask a police officer or information person for help

I0541480

Be
Safe!

3

Everywhere We Go in This Book

You can also see where all of the above sites are located on the map on Pg. 36

ROCKET AROUND *Washington DC!*

Written by
Lee Lynch

Illustrations by
Emma Lynch

Contributors
Jeffrey, Jack, & Tom Lynch

ROCKET AROUND LLC   U.S.A.

This book is for neurodiverse kids of any age, who love adventure, imagination, and finding new ways to have fun!

Neurodiverse people behave, think, and learn differently from people with neurotypical brains. These differences include strengths. In a word, neurodiverse people are awesome. Neurodiverse people might be autistic, live with ADHD, dyslexia, PTSD, Tourette's, or other things.

Everywhere We Go continued

See page 40 to be a ROCKETAROUNDER!

Hello human friends!

My name is Rocket the travel pug.

I love to visit cool new places.

Adventure is one of my favorite things (behind humans and sleep).

You too? Great! Let's travel together!

Today my human family is going to the District of Columbia, also known as Washington DC or just DC. It's the capital of the United States.

I love being at home with my fabulous human family -- Mom, Dad, Jeffrey, Jack, and Emma. Here are their pictures.

But I also LOVE seeing new places. DC is not far from my house. I just know they are taking me with them! They wouldn't leave ME behind, right?

They're zipping up their backpacks so we must be leaving.

And they are out the door!

Wait – what about me? They must not know they left me behind.

I'll try the back door...Hi-ya! I am out!!

Now, where did they go? Sniff, sniff - I smell them! Come with me!

They hopped on the Metro train to go into the city. We will too.

We're probably not supposed to be on here alone, so we'll just hide under this Metro seat.

The train stopped. Sniff, sniff - my humans got off here, at Arlington National Cemetery.

Since 1864, it's been a cemetery and today it has gravesites for more than 14,000 veterans.

There's so much to see here, so it's great that there's a tram that goes all around the cemetery.

Let's go inside. OH NO – NO DOGS ALLOWED! Sniff, sniff. Smells like my humans are heading this way.

What to See

The graves of American heroes who have served America, such as former Presidents William Howard Taft and John F. Kennedy.

It also has the Tomb of the Unknown Soldier, which has the remains of unknown soldiers from World War I, World War II, and the Korean War, and a sculpture honoring servicewomen and dogs.

Arlington National Cemetery

They're at the Lincoln Memorial – one of the most beautiful monuments in a city full of monuments!

More than seven million people visit here every year. It sits at one end of what's called the National Mall – a huge open area of memorials, museums, and even pools of water -- stretching to the U.S. Capitol.

Inside, it has a giant statue of Abraham (Abe) Lincoln, the 16th U.S. president who led America through the Civil War.

Lincoln Memorial

What to See

The words from two of President Lincoln's most famous speeches -- the Gettysburg Address and his address after he was elected President a second time – are inscribed on the walls in big letters.

Can you read them out loud? Great job!

Uh oh - I've lost my humans' scent.

Time to move on!

Sniff, sniff. Over here! They walked through the Vietnam Veterans Memorial. It's different than other memorials on the National Mall. You can see your reflection in the shiny black wall that is in the shape of a 'V', with one side stretching toward the Lincoln Memorial and the other side toward the Washington Monument.

Then they went over to the Korean War Veterans Memorial.

Vietnam Veterans Memorial

These are really cool things, but where are my humans??

Sniff, sniff. They went this way.

Korean War Memorial

The Vietnam Veterans Memorial lists the names of the more than 58,000 Americans who died serving in the Vietnam War (1959-1975).

The Korean War Veterans Memorial is dedicated to the women and men who served in the armed forces during the Korean War (1951 – 1953), including those who died serving. The memorial is created in a way that makes it seem like, no matter where you stand, at least one of the soldiers is looking at you.

What to See

The columns at the National World War II Memorial stand for the role that U.S. states and territories played in winning the war.

There are two engravings of "Kilroy was here" in the memorial. Kilroy is a doodle that soldiers use to draw on places. If you're at the memorial, can you find Kilroy?

It's the National World War II Memorial, honoring the 16 million people who served America during World War II (1939 – 1945).

It's amazing – 56 columns in a semi-circle around a beautiful fountain and pool (so refreshing). Yikes - I've lost my family's scent! They walked over here.

World War II Memorial

To the [White House](#) – where the President and his family live! Every president has lived and worked here while serving as president since John Adams in 1800. It's bigger than it looks.

It has six stories, 132 rooms, and a huge lawn for the presidential dogs. Lucky pups! You can go inside for tours, but it smells like my humans have moved on.

Rocket ar the White House

What to See

At the White House: 35 bathrooms, 28 fireplaces, three elevators, a movie theater, a tennis court, a jogging track, a swimming pool, and a putting green.

The White House also has 147 windows - all bulletproof!

A big fire set by British troops damaged a lot of it in 1814, but it's been repaired.

I think they came over here to the [Washington Monument](), honoring America's first president, George Washington. It sits at the center of the Mall. Man is that TALL!

It reminds me of one of my other favorite things – a really big stick. If only I could get my mouth around it.

Wait – what am I doing? I need to find my humans. Sniff, sniff - smells like history.

What to See

The Washington Monument is the tallest building on the National Mall.

Sometimes the elevator inside is open and you can go to the top.

Washington Monument

They're in the [National Museum of American History](#)! Finding them in there will be tricky. NO DOGS ALLOWED! Time to get sneaky.

I'll get into this kid's backpack and strike my best, stuffed animal pose.

I'm in!

Look - it's the original Star-Spangled Banner flag, Abe Lincoln's top hat, and Dorothy's ruby slippers from The Wizard of Oz.

There are even video games!

I'll bet my humans are with the video games.

What to See

The first computer bug and an exhibit on how cars, buses, trains, and airplanes helped America grow.

Plus there are lots of kids' technology activities.

National Museum of American History

Oh no!

I think they've left.

They're here at the [National Children's Museum](#)!

Oh brother – there's that sign again – NO DOGS ALLOWED! Time to get sneaky.

I'll climb up this pole, go across the roof, climb onto the ceiling, and go down the three-story slide – WOO HOO!

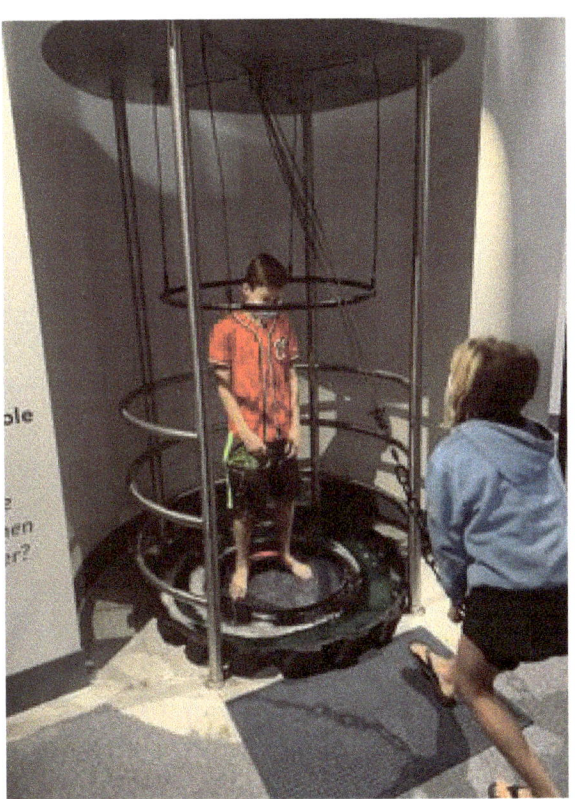

They have everything here -- climbing contraptions, a giant bubble-making machine, a science alley, virtual games, building blocks. Where do I start!

What to See

The National Children's Museum has endless activities: Finding my superpower, practicing baseball hitting and pitching, air basketball, model car racing, a wall to measure how high you can touch while jumping, a craft studio, a giant video screen, and more.

National Children's Museum

Hold on - Sniff, sniff. I'm losing my humans' scent. Gotta go!

They're headed toward the [National Archives Building](#), where America's Charters of Freedom – the original Declaration of Independence, U.S. Constitution, and Bill of Rights - are on display. NO DOGS ALLOWED! Dog-gone.

Now they're headed through the [National Gallery of Art Sculpture Garden](#) and still going.

At the *Archives* - original papers, letters, and stories of the amendments to the U.S. Constitution, and of the struggles Americans faced to gain rights. At the *Sculpture Garden* - six acres of giant modern sculptures – even a giant spider sculpture! In the middle is a fountain that's an ice-skating rink in the winter.

National Archives

Sculpture Garden

They went to the [National Museum of Natural History](#). I love that place - so much in there about animals. We'll just head on in - NO DOGS ALLOWED? Are you kidding? If I were stuffed, they'd put me on display!

Time to get sneaky. If I stay low to the ground, I can back in through the exit as people are walking out.

Whew! I almost got stepped on. The giant whale and mega-toothed shark display hanging from the ceiling are kind of freaking me out.

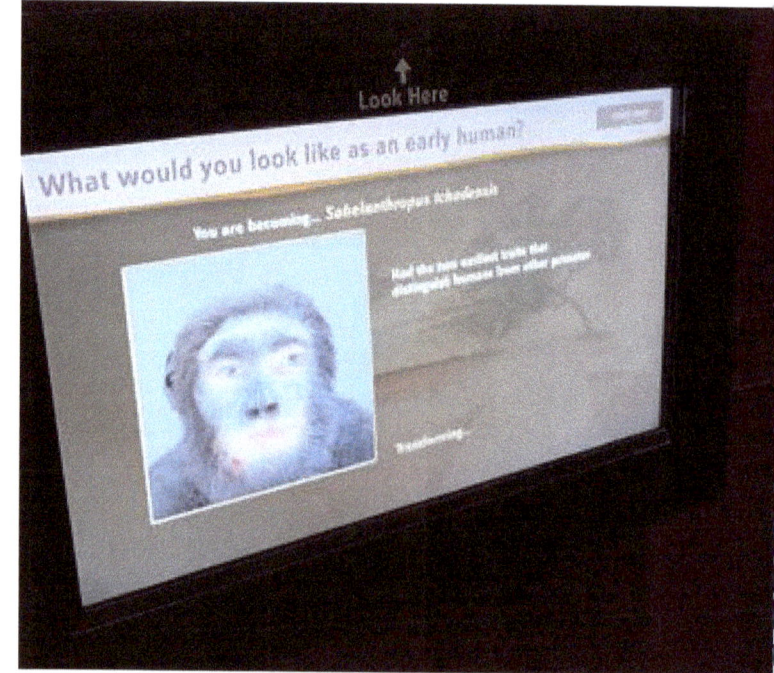

What to See

National Museum of Natural History

The huge stuffed African elephant in the middle is really cool. And the exhibits are amazing – oceans, mummies from ancient Egypt, mammals – like early and wild dogs (dingos), a butterfly pavilion, a live insect zoo, and gems, minerals, and rocks. There's even a video game display where you can save the world from a dangerous virus.

I love the dinosaur bones exhibit! How can I take one of those home to bury in my yard? I wonder if they're here in the Human Origins exhibit. Look -- it's a picture on the screen of what Jack would look like as an early human! They've got to be nearby!

What to See

[James Smithson](#) (1765-1829) was an English scientist who loved learning and wanted to increase knowledge among humans. He never made it to the U.S., but he left all of his money to create the Smithsonian Institution, which today includes 19 museums, 21 libraries, nine research centers, and a zoo. Most are located in Washington DC and many are free to enter.

There they are - heading out the door and over toward a big red building called the [Smithsonian Visitor Center](#). It's called the castle because it looks like one. Hmmm - it smells like my humans have been on the [Carousel on the Mall](#) – all horse except for one sea dragon. It's the only carousel in DC.

Oh geez – they've moved on.

Smithsonian "Castle"

Carousel

Speaking of Smithsonian museums, my humans headed to the National Museum of African American History and Culture. It's all about African American life, history, and culture.

Museum of African American History

It's a great place to visit, but my humans have moved on to the National Portrait Gallery and the National Gallery of Art.

The National Portrait Gallery – another Smithsonian museum – has America's only full collection of presidential portraits outside of the White House.

The National Gallery of Art has more than 140,000 pieces of art created over hundreds of years. It might take them a while to get through there. Some of the pieces of art are of dogs, like me!

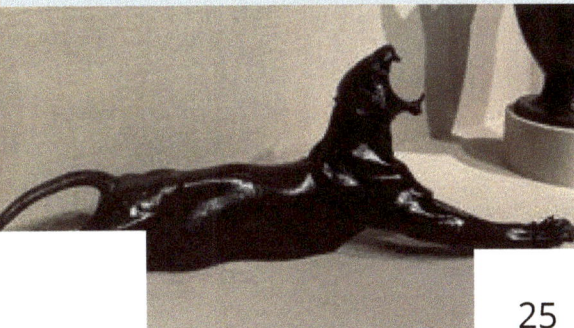

National Gallery of Art

Now, they're heading to the [National Air and Space Museum](#)! And once again NO DOGS ALLOWED. This does not make sense -- my collar tag says ROCKET!!!

Okay, I'll squeeze in between these nice humans and we'll all cruise into the museum together - we're in!

The Smithsonian National Air and Space Museum has the world's largest collection of aviation and space artifacts. It's one of America's most visited museums.

They have everything about flight in here.

Sniff, sniff - no idea why my humans are moving on from the Air and Space, but there they go!

EVERYTHING! Information about U.S. space missions to the moon and the planets!

Giant telescopes, astronomy, navigation, and time-keeping devices, plus one of the planes built by the Wright brothers - the first to invent, build, and fly the first airplane with a motor. So many ROCKETS here!! They even have a statue of Sydney the dog explorer.

If you're at the museum, make sure you fly a rocket simulator - it goes upside down!

National Air and Space Museum

What to See

The National Museum of the American Indian is one of the world's largest collections of Native pieces telling the story of the history and lives of American Indians.

The U.S. Botanic Garden is a living plant museum and the oldest constantly operating botanic garden in the U.S. If you're at the garden, how many different colors of flowers do you see?

They went into the National Museum of the American Indian. Can't wait to go inside. Oh no, my humans are moving on!

Museum of the American Indian

Pocahontas didn't save John Smith. She saved America.

They are heading to the U.S. Botanic Garden. So many plants and flowers - I just love to sniff them all.

But what I do not smell here are my humans.

U.S. Botanical Gardens

he [U.S. Capitol](#) is right across the treet - they must be heading there. ou can't miss it – its dome and the tatue of Lady Freedom on top are opular images representing merica's democratic form of overnment.

nd it has another refreshing eflecting pool in front of it. Maybe I'll st cool off in there. Oh no – just hen things were getting interesting, smells like my humans moved on.

What to See

It's a cool place because of how it looks and what's usually happening inside. Since the year 1800, the U.S. Congress has met here to discuss the business of the American people.

The dome shape of [Statuary Hall](#) creates a sound effect where you can stand yards away and hear someone whispering. If you're at the Capitol, try it!

U.S. Capitol and reflecting pool

What to See

Inside are millions of books, photographs, newspapers, and other media and documents. It has the world's largest law library of books, music, and motion pictures. It already has more than 170 million items, and every day it adds another 10,000 pieces. What's your favorite book? If you're at the Library, is it there?

They went into the [Library of Congress] – the biggest library in the world. This is where researchers for Congress find information.

I hope my humans aren't going to try to read EVERYTHING in here. Smells like they're heading somewhere else.

The Gutenberg Bible

They went into the [National Postal Museum](#) – the old post office building for the city of Washington DC. It has amazing displays about postal history and "philately", or the study of postage stamps.

You can do fun things here - even make a virtual collection of dog stamps! My favorite display is of Owney, the Railway Mail Service mascot dog (1887 – 1897) who rode the mail rail cars for most of his life! Wait - is that my human family back on the bus?! Come on!

Whew – that bus moves fast! They got off here, at the [International Spy Museum](), the perfect place for a pup with my sneakiness! It's not going to be easy to sneak in. Alright – I'll go up onto the roof, down the air duct, and drop into the car of the world's most famous movie spy, James Bond. YES - I'm in.

It's the largest collection on international 'espionage' (fancy word for spying) in the world. Sniff, sniff - my humans are on the move again.

What to See

You can get your undercover assignment then do all kinds of super-fun spy activities.

You can see tons of spy gadgets and check out famous spies and their tricks.

You can even try cracking codes.

Hurry - they're back on the bus! But I'm close behind. There it goes past the [Jefferson Memorial](#), a beautiful dome structure in honor of Thomas Jefferson (1743 – 1826). Now it's going around the Tidal Basin - such a beautiful view!

What to See

In Spring, the more than 3,700 cherry trees around the Jefferson Memorial and Tidal Basin are covered with beautiful white flowers that look like little snowballs.

Jefferson Memorial (on top) and Tidal Basin

But there's no time to stop - the bus is heading past the Martin Luther King Jr. Memorial (MLK Jr.), Franklin Delano Roosevelt Memorial (FDR) (awww - there's Preident Roosevelt's dog Fala), and the Kennedy Center, and it's going toward Memorial Bridge.

That must mean my human family is heading home! Uh oh – I need to get home fast. My humans will worry if I'm not there.

MLK Jr. Memorial (at left) and FDR Memorial (below)

The fastest way home is to hop on the Metro, cut through the yards in my neighborhood, scratch on the door, and sneak past the dog walker as she opens it.

Whew – that was close! My humans are so happy to see me but they don't know how lucky they were to have me watching out for them all day!

It was GREAT rocketing around DC with you! I don't know about you, but it wore me out.

Now it's time for one of my other favorite things - sleeping.

Catch you on our next adventure, after some

zzzzzzzzzzzzzzzzzzzzzzzzzzzzzzz's

The National Mall & Downtown Washington DC

Match the numbers to the sites on the next page.

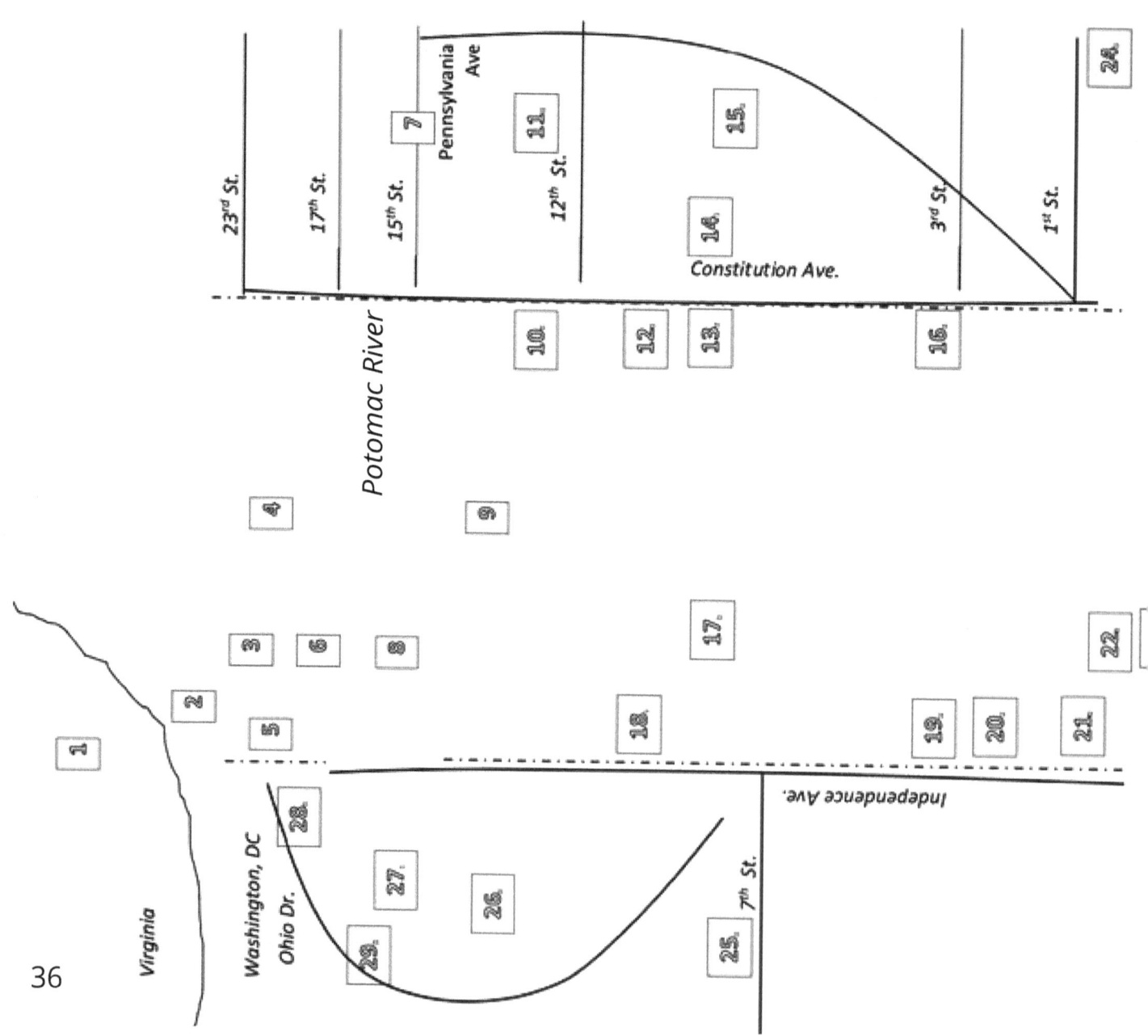

What's on The Map

1. Arlington National Cemetery
2. Memorial Bridge
3. Lincoln Memorial
4. Vietnam Memorial
5. Korean War Veterans Memorial
6. National World War II Memorial
7. The White House
8. Washington Monument
9. National Museum of African American History and Culture
10. National Museum of American History
11. National Children's Museum
12. National Museum of Natural History
13. National Gallery of Art Sculpture Garden
14. National Archives Building
15. National Portrait Gallery
16. National Gallery of Art
17. Carousel on the Mall
18. Smithsonian 'castle' (Smithsonian Institution Building)
19. National Air and Space Museum
20. National Museum of the American Indian
21. U.S. Botanic Garden
22. United States Capitol
23. Library of Congress
24. National Postal Museum
25. International Spy Museum
26. Jefferson Memorial
27. Tidal Basin
28. MLK (Martin Luther King) Memorial
29. FDR (Franklin Delano Roosevelt) Memorial

- - - - - - - - - - - - - - - -
The National Mall
- - - - - - - - - - - - - - - -

Note: Most streets do not appear on the map.

What Else to See When You Rocket around DC
Check each one you would like to see!

___ Paddle boats on the Tidal Basin
___ African American Civil War Memorial
___ Bureau of Engraving and Printing
___ Chinatown
___ DC United men's soccer game
___ DC Waterfront (District Wharf)
___ DC World War I Memorial
___ Eastern Market
___ Eisenhower Memorial
___ Emancipation Memorial
___ Freedom Plaza
___ Food and ice cream trucks
___ Ford's Theater
___ Lockkeeper's House, Washington Monument
___ Japanese American National Museum
___ Hirshhorn Museum and Sculpture Gallery
___ National Building Museum
___ National Cathedral
___ National Geographic Museum
___ National Shrine
___ National Women's History Museum

O Museum at the Mansion ___
Smithsonian National Zoo ___
The Corcoran Art Gallery ___
The Folger ___
The Shakespeare Theatre ___
The Supreme Court ___
The Willard Hotel ___
Union Station ___
US Navy War Memorial ___
US National Arboretum ___
Vietnam Women's Memorial ___
Washington Capitals hockey game ___
Washington Commanders football game (Maryland) ___
Washington Mystics women's basketball game ___
Washington Nationals baseball game ___
Washington Spirit women's soccer game ___
Washington Wizards men's basketball game ___
US Holocaust Memorial Museum ___

Be a Rocketarounder!

1. Share Rocket's values of building your brain through adventure, imagination, and finding new ways to have fun!

2. Read *Rocket Around Washington DC.* Which Rocket Around books have you read? Write them here: _____

_____

3. Where should Rocket and his humans go next? Where would your dog want to rocket around with Rocket? Email your ideas to Rocket at lee@rocketaround.com (make sure your mom or dad is okay with it first).

<u>Congratulations, you are an</u> <u>official Rocketarounder - welcome to the Club!</u>

I'M A ROCKETAROUNDER!
I build my brain through:
-*Adventure*
-*Imagination*
-*Finding new ways to have fun!*

The Humans + Rocket

Rocket is real, and he lives with his awesome (his word, not ours) neurodiverse family in Alexandria, VA.

They love seeing new things, traveling, reading, writing, sports, music, chess, anime, chewing sticks and toys, and sleeping.

They hope you enjoyed this book and that you'll read the next one!

ISBN: 979-8-9889331-2-0
Text copyright 2023.
Illustrations copyright 2023.
All rights reserved. Published by Rocket Around LLC.
Printed in the U.S.A.

Rocket Around books:
Rocket Around Washington DC - A Neurodiverse Visual Guide for Kids
Rocket Around Washington DC - A Neurodiverse Activities and Coloring Book
Rocket Around Washington DC eBook

Look for these books and other fun kids' activities at rocketaround.com

www.ingramcontent.com/pod-product-compliance
Lightning Source LLC
Chambersburg PA
CBHW041525120626
46551CB00018B/2572